THE
ANGRY BIRDS™
MOVIE

GUIDE BOOK
BY CHRIS CERASI

centum

ANGRY BIRDS MOVIE: GUIDE BOOK
A CENTUM BOOK 978-1-910916-22-3

First published in the United States by HarperFestival,
an imprint of HarperCollins Children's Books 2016.

Published in Great Britain by Centum Books Ltd
Centum Books Ltd, 20 Devon Square,
Newton Abbot, Devon, TQ12 2HR, UK
books@centumbooksltd.co.uk
CENTUM BOOKS Limited Reg. No. 07641486

This edition published 2016

A CIP catalogue record
for this book is available
from the British Library.

Printed in China

1 3 5 7 9 10 8 6 4 2

CONTENTS

SECTION 1

99% ANGRY

Oh, ah. Hi there. Um, so . . . My name is Red. I'm apparently an "angry bird", but if you ask me, everyone else is so dang cheerful all the time that anything less than a beak-splitting grin is considered angry! Anyway, as part of my anger-management training, I've been asked to be your guide through Bird Island. Normally that pink bundle of annoying energy named Stella would be your guide, but I don't have much of a choice. So let's just get this over with so I can go back to being with my favourite person (myself) and doing what I love best (which – you guessed it – is being left alone!).

But before we get started, please just keep one thing in mind. Think of this as one of Red's Rules: *Some birds are born to be angry.*

So, uh, yeah, welcome to the world of the Angry Birds. Try not to ask too many questions, OK?

BIRD ISLAND

Bird Island is in the middle of a vast sea. It's a big place, full of dense jungles, large mountains, sandy beaches, waterfalls, green forests and rocky cliffs. It has every environment a bird could want, plus the weather is almost always sunny and nice. Don't tell Stella I said this, but it's pretty much the most

JUNGLE

BEACH

beautiful place I have ever lived. It's also the *only* place I have ever lived, but, whatever. It's my home, and it's the best home a bird could ask for.

I live on the island with – you guessed it – my fellow birds. I'm supposed to say that we're a happy, carefree bunch and that's basically true of almost every bird. I'm not unhappy, mind you. I'm just not particularly all-the-time happy. But at the end of the day, I really am glad I live in such a beautiful place. Here's a map with a few special spots labelled, in case you want to explore.

See, that was almost cheerful, wasn't it?

MIGHTY EAGLE'S SECRET MOUNTAIN LAIR
– APPROXIMATE LOCATION
(YOU KNOW WHAT A *SECRET* IS, RIGHT?)

FOREST

BIRD VILLAGE

7

RED

I guess I should tell you a little about myself. Normally I am a very private bird, but since I had to take anger-management classes, I don't have much of a choice. Here's a test I took during class. A lot of birds have taken it – for fun. It's supposed to help us get in touch with our inner songbirds. Whatever. Here are my answers.

ALL ABOUT RED

OCCUPATION: Wanting to be left alone!

FAVOURITE COLOUR: Red, duh.

FAVOURITE BOOK: Any Mighty Eagle comic book that I can read by myself in my own hut, thankyouverymuch!

SPECIAL SKILLS: I am very good at spending time ALONE.

HOBBIES: Being alone. Pretty much doing anything alone.

FAVOURITE PLACE ON BIRD ISLAND: My own hut.

BEST FRIEND: Me. Well, I guess Chuck is pretty cool. And Bomb. But don't tell them I said so.

GREATEST WISH: To be left alone.

BIGGEST FEAR: Being hugged.

WHAT MAKES YOU HAPPY? Privacy.

WHAT MAKES YOU ANGRY? Being asked all these questions! And slow-moving birds. And loud birds. And late birds. And spoiled birds. And cheerful birds. And birds who stand too close. And birds who complain. And cheerful birds. And that bird who likes to give hugs. And birds who don't respect personal space. And birds who make me do anger management. And cheerful birds. Oh, and did I mention birds who are so dang cheerful that it starts TO MAKE ME ANGRY, and also EVERY BIRD AND THING AND PLACE ON THIS ISLAND?!

MOTTO: Keep to yourself. It's better that way.

A Great Way to Start Your Day

My hut is on the beach, far away from everyone else's (which is how I like it), so the paper delivery almost always comes later in the morning, which tends to make me a bit angry. But if I wanted my paper earlier, I'd have to live closer to the other birds, which is definitely NOT going to happen. *The Daily Peep* is the only newspaper on Bird Island. Take a gander and see if there are any island events you want to attend (or avoid). *The Daily Peep* is pretty informative, even though I've been featured in it a few times, and they've made me out to be some sort of recluse with a bad attitude.

Anyway, breakfast and *The Daily Peep* are how I start my day. Then I work on my plans for my dream hut – something even bigger and more private than the one I am currently living in.

YOU'RE ON ISLAND TIME NOW, SO DO LIKE I DO: EASE INTO THE DAY.

DREAM NEST MODEL

CALMING OCEAN VIEW

INDOOR/OUTDOOR BATH FOR PRIVATE BATHING

STAIRS TO MY PERSONAL SANCTUARY

The Daily Peep

Raving Red Battles Boisterous Beach Birds

A certain red bird runs the risk of becoming Bird Island's resident party pooper as his foul temper ruins another bird-day party days after the first, now-infamous Bird-Day Blow-Up.

Sources say that Red, a resident of Bird Island Beach, became enraged when noise from a nearby bird-day celebration grew too loud and disturbed his privacy and peace. It is unclear when the partygoers arrived and began their festivities, but apparently they

were partying too closely and too loudly for Red's comfort. And as each errant beach ball bounced against Red's hut, his anger escalated.

An anonymous witness says the final blow – a beach ball to the head – set off Red's spectacular temper explosion. He began kicking sand everywhere and squawking loudly about his space being invaded.

"It was terrible," said one of the party attendees. "Red just came running out of his house and began yelling. All we were doing was celebrating my friend Gus's twelfth bird-day with cake, games and a few noisemakers. He just turned into a red orb of anger! The way he screamed at us and carried on, you would think we had tossed fireworks inside his hut." When pressed, this party-goer admitted that quite a few beach balls had rico-cheted off of Red's home and that the partyers may have targeted the hut once the recluse started confis-cating the inflatable ob-jects.

When reached for com-ment, Red refused to leave his house and would only shout "Go away!" behind his closed door. It is un-clear if this latest outburst will impact the terms of Red's court-sanctioned anger-management classes. But all of Bird Island hopes that one day soon this extremely angry bird will change his ways.

BIRD VILLAGE

Almost all the birds of Bird Island live in the area known as Bird Village. This is where many birds work, shop, relax, eat and do just about everything else. Main Street runs right through the middle of the village. It's the epicentre of bird culture and life. Because this is where everything

is happening, it's also a popular place to hang out. So you *might* run into me in town. It would be better if there weren't so many other birds around and *so* much better if only the birds I liked lived there. But I guess it takes more than three birds to make a village.

DOWN ON MAIN STREET

Bird Village has a lot of interesting shops and businesses. Even though I avoid these places, you'll probably enjoy making a few stops while strolling down Main Street. Here are a few standouts for food, fun and learning about life on Bird Island.

EARLY BIRD WORMS

This is the best place to get the most delicious worms in the whole of Bird Village. The owner imports them from all over the island. Like the name says, you have to get here pretty early in the day to get the choicest worms. It means having to wait in a long line with some of the most annoying . . . uh, that is, *lively* birds in the village. Who tend to stand real close. So set your alarm clocks and get ready to fill a big bucket of the juiciest, finest worms. Then head to the park for a picnic.

LATE RISER WORMS

This is the worst place to get worms in the whole of Bird Village, unless you like your worms skinny, chewy and stale. The bird who runs this shop is a heck of a bird. But he just gets up too late and ends up with all the rejected worms from the Early Bird! There's always a small line outside his shop and it's usually made up of those birds who just can't seem to get their feathers together.

EARLY BIRD
WORMS

LATE RISER
WORMS

SORRY
No WORMS
TODAY

THE EXCLUSIVE BATH

THE BIRD BATH

The Bird Bath is a must-see destination for most birds when it's warm and sunny – which is almost every day on Bird Island. Do you like to cool off while conversing with other birds, or splash around in style? Either way, be prepared for crowds at the hottest spot for chilling out.

THE BIRD BATH ENTRANCE

BIRD DAY CARE CENTRE

This is a place I usually walk by as fast as I can. You have to be . . . well, everything I'm not in order to work there! Patient, understanding, nurturing . . . patient. Listen, I know my flaws, OK?

Still, for those who have children, this really is a great place to bring unhatched birdlings, as the birds here are "trained to take the very best care of your precious cargo, surrounding them with love, personal attention and only positive energy".

OK, I just read all of that from the brochure. So sue me.

HUG TRADER

Oh boy, *this guy*. He trades in hugs, just like his store name says. He stands outside his shop and gives hugs to any bird who looks slightly interested! Every time I walk by, he looks at me expecting a hug, and every time my answer is the same: nuh-uh! No way. NOT going to happen. Nope. No, no and no.

NAP BAR

Who doesn't love a good nap at least once or twice a day? For the bird on the go, this is the best place to catch up on some much-needed rest. The hammocks are super-comfy, and the soft island breeze gently lulls you to sleep. Sweet dreams are guaranteed.

BIRDS OF A FEATHER SALON

There are a lot of fashionable birds on Bird Island, and they all go to Birds of a Feather Salon to get their feathers done in style. Curled, dyed, streaked, teased, trimmed, fluffed, you name it. There is always a crowd there, and it's a constant flurry of activity. Birds talking, birds laughing, birds cooing with delight.

I'll be honest. I tried going there once and it really wasn't for me. I personally prefer to clip my own feathers, as that way I don't have to listen to any silly conversations or deal with any other . . . anything. But Chuck swears by them, so, go figure.

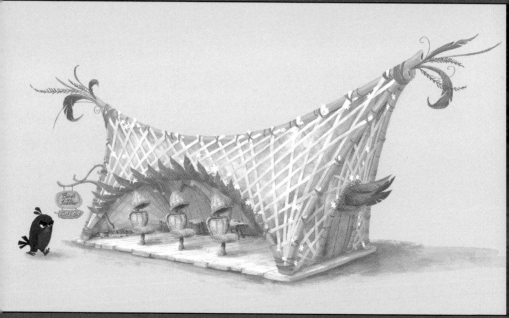

BIRDFEEDER RESTAURANT

Feathers-down, the Birdfeeder is the fanciest restaurant in Bird Village. It prides itself on locally sourcing the freshest ingredients from all over Bird Island. The fruit du jour is something to behold. And since the menu changes all the time, you're always in for a surprise. They put on great shows as well, so it's no wonder that you'll find a crowd there almost every night. The staff is also very accommodating. They always find a table for one if a bird happens to be flying solo.

BIRD ISLAND POLICE STATION

Even though you'll likely never have to go to the police station, it's worth knowing about – just in case you are an eyewitness to a minor altercation between a few rowdy partygoers and an innocent-until-proven-guilty beachcomber. So stop by for a quick "hello" when you're in the village.

THE WEEKLY BIRD ISLAND POLICE BLOTTER

Angry outburst in the diner -
subject and bystanders questioned

Angry outburst at the movies -
subject and bystanders questioned

Speeding ticket -
ticket issued

Unexplained detonation in the park -
bystanders questioned, still under investigation

Angry outburst at the beach -
subject and bystanders questioned

BIRD COURT

Bird Court is the source of justice and law and rules and all that ... stuff. It is presided over by Judge Peckinpah, whose alleged wisdom and judgement keep Bird Island safe and secure. So he claims. All the time!

You can attend hearings anytime. And all birds must serve jury duty, so every chirp is heard and counted. Clearly something is working, since the island is such a peaceful place – most of the time for most of the birds. It's just difficult for birds who are repeat "guests" of the court to feel peaceful – *especially* if they are sentenced to anger-management classes.

But everyone agrees on one thing: the statue of Mighty Eagle that looms large in the background is a real shot in the wing. Mighty Eagle watches over all of Bird Island. His bravery and nobility are legendary. Just looking up at the majestic statue can soothe and inspire the angriest of birds.

BIRD COURT

Infinity Acceptance Centre

Last we come to the bane of my existence – I mean, one of Bird Village's most fascinating places: the Infinity Acceptance Centre, run by former Angry Bird Matilda. Everyone is welcome, especially those found to be a little too angry or stressed or antisocial. Attendees are forced – I mean *encouraged* – to discover inner peace and become better birds. A recovered Angry Bird, Matilda is now the foremost authority on what it means to be the most ideal bird. Through yoga, meditation and painting, birds strive to find ideal means of expression and . . . Oh geez, I just can't. . . . This is killing me. I don't know about you, but I'm exhausted. Let's call it a day for now, OK? I gotta get out of here.

TOP 10 THINGS TO AVOID ON BIRD ISLAND
HERE IS A LIST OF THE TEN THINGS THAT CURRENTLY GET MY FEATHERS IN A FLUFF!

1. **BIRD COURT:** It's where I found myself sentenced to anger-management classes after a perfectly reasonable misunderstanding between me and a family at a bird-day party. That Judge Peckinpah is a MONSTER, I tell you!

2. **MATILDA'S ANGER-MANAGEMENT CLASS:** Hippie-dippy Matilda loves to "reform" Angry Birds, but if you ask me, her yolk is all scrambled.

3. **LATE RISER WORMS:** If you snooze, you lose at this place. Sleep in and run the risk of having the most unsatisfying meal on the island.

4. **BIRD DAY CARE CENTRE:** Imagine having to take care of all those unhatched birdlings?! I shudder just thinking about it.

5. **CENTRAL BIRD PARK:** All those birds having fun and being loud all around you, spoiling your peace and quiet? NO THANK YOU!

6. BIRD DOCTOR: Going to the doctor is no fun, especially if it involves a busted beak or a sprained wing. I try to stay safe at all times so I never wind up there. Although the birds there DO take good care of us, so I guess I shouldn't grumble. Much.

7. HUG TRADER: What kind of deranged bird WANTS to give and get hugs all the time?! As far as I am concerned, that is NOT normal!

8. THE BIRDFEEDER RESTAURANT: But only when the early-bird special is being served. It may be good for business, but it's not good for a peaceful dining experience.

9. POLICE STATION: Not that there's much crime on Bird Island, but you want to stay on the good side of these official birds. Trust me.

10. BIRDS OF A FEATHER SALON: I like my feathers trimmed just so, but I cannot tell you how many times these nitwits have taken too much off the top! They also take for ever because their beaks never stop flapping!

BIRDS AT WORK

Ever wonder where you would work if you lived on Bird Island?
Answer the questions below to see what your dream job would be.

WHICH OF THE FOLLOWING SOUNDS LIKE THE MOST FUN TO YOU?

A Reading storybooks to lots of sweet baby hatchlings.
B Serving up creative juicy worm salads to hungry customers.
C Making sure everyone has a chance for a nice, long afternoon nap.
D Reporting on interesting stories from all over the city.
E Teaching birds how to be calm, creative and centred.

WHAT DO YOU THINK SOUNDS THE MOST FUN TO WEAR TO WORK?

A A soft T-shirt, so you can sit and work in comfort.
B An apron to protect your feathers while you create food masterpieces.
C A stopwatch to time things precisely.
D A hat with a sign that says PRESS on it.
E A bracelet made of beads and string.

WHICH OF THE FOLLOWING CHALLENGES SOUNDS MOST APPEALING TO YOU?

A Helping to care for and shape the future generation.
B Getting in the kitchen and experimenting with recipes.
C Making sure everyone is rested, healthy and content.
D Asking lots of questions and doing lots of investigating.
E Helping others control their anger and find inner peace.

WHO WOULD YOU WANT TO HAVE AS LOYAL CUSTOMERS?

A Unhatched birdlings warm and cosy in their shells.
B Hungry birds eager to try your latest food masterpiece.
C Sleepy birds who can't wait to curl up for a really nice, long nap.
D Avid readers who can't wait to read all the latest news.
E Angry and stressed-out birds who need guidance and calm.

WHAT IS YOUR FAVOURITE TIME TO WORK?

A Mornings and afternoons only, while busy parents are at work.
B Breakfast, lunch and dinner, as I love being in the kitchen!
C Late mornings and mid-afternoons only.
D Around the clock – the news never sleeps!
E In the morning after a nice, healthy breakfast.

So what's your Bird Island job?!

If you answered A to most of the questions, you are a caretaker at the Bird Day Care Centre.
If you answered B to most of the questions, you are a chef at the Birdfeeder Restaurant.
If you answered C to most of the questions, you are an attendant at the Nap Bar.
If you answered D to most of the questions, you are a reporter for *The Daily Peep*.
If you answered E to most of the questions, you are an instructor at the Infinity Acceptance Centre.

POP QUIZ!
Island Life

I hope you've been paying attention, because I'm going to ask you all about island life. Don't make me look bad, OK, or I'll have to go to another one of Matilda's classes.

1. WHAT IS THE NAME OF MY FAVOURITE CAFÉ?

2. WHO IS THE JUDGE THAT PRESIDES OVER BIRD COURT?

3. WHO IS THE GREATEST BIRD OF ALL TIME, DEFENDER OF BIRD ISLAND?

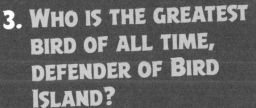

4. I GUESS I SORT-OF-KIND-OF-OK-YEAH HAVE TWO BEST FRIENDS. WHAT ARE THEIR NAMES?

5. WHAT IS THE NAME OF BIRD ISLAND'S BEST (AND ONLY) NEWSPAPER?

6. WHO RUNS THE INFINITY ACCEPTANCE CENTRE (AND IS MAKING MY LIFE MISERABLE)?

7. WHERE IS THE BEST PLACE TO GET WORMS IN BIRD VILLAGE?

8. WHERE IS THE BEST PLACE TO GET YOUR FEATHERS TRIMMED?

9. TRUE OR FALSE:

I have lived in many places other than Bird Island.

10. TRUE OR FALSE:

The Hug Trader is my favourite place to go in Bird Village.

ANSWER KEY:

1. The Birdfeeder Restaurant 2. Peckinpah 3. Mighty Eagle 4. Chuck and Bomb 5. *The Daily Peep* 6. Matilda 7. Early Bird Worms 8. Birds of a Feather Salon 9. False 10. False

37

SECTION 2

MEET THE FLOCK

Sure Bird Island is beautiful and the shops are interesting. But the heart and soul of the island are - you guessed it - the birds. I either know them personally or have had, uh, dealings with them, but they are all essential parts of Bird Village. Ready for another one of Red's Rules? *Happy birds are too busy being happy to notice anything around them other than their own silly needs.* Do you want the happy? Can you handle the happy? Now is the time to find out.

JUDGE PECKINPAH

Judge Peckinpah loves three things most of all: the sound of his own voice, holding court – even when he's not actually in court – and sentencing birds to horrible things like daily anger-management classes at the Infinity Acceptance Centre.

He can be seen strutting around Bird Village like he owns the place. The judge is so small that underneath his robes, he stands on the shoulders of another bird, Cyrus. But every bird knows the truth, so he's not fooling any of us. Judge Peckinpah believes he's answering a higher calling – one that requires a higher perch – on Cyrus's shoulders!

CYRUS

Cyrus, the judge's perch, has the worst job on Bird Island. If that isn't bad enough, he also suffers from terrible allergies, so he's constantly sneezing. Despite the daily dose of propping up Peckinpah and his never-ending allergies, Cyrus is extremely happy and carefree. I can't wrap my bird brain around that.

ALL ABOUT JUDGE PECKINPAH

OCCUPATION: Why, judge of Bird Court, of course.

FAVOURITE COLOUR: Brown, the colour of my hammer and the symbol of justice!

FAVOURITE BOOK: *The Basic Book of Bird Justice and Law*, Volumes 1–27. They are never far from my reach, since a few volumes make a good booster seat.

SPECIAL SKILLS: Dispensing the law, justice, authority and equality all throughout the land!

HOBBIES: Judging. Golfing.

FAVOURITE PLACE ON BIRD ISLAND: Bird Court, where else?

BEST FRIEND: Truth and justice. Oh, and I guess Cyrus, too.

GREATEST WISH: Justice for all.

BIGGEST FEAR: Being looked down upon by other birds.

WHAT MAKES YOU HAPPY? Dispensing the law, justice, authority and equality all throughout the land!

WHAT MAKES YOU ANGRY? Disorder caused by Angry Birds.

MOTTO: Be the hammer of justice (or something just as heavy).

Stella

Stella is one of the happiest and most optimistic birds around. Her pink feathers and constant smile make her popular with *almost* everyone. Occasionally her perky behaviour ruffles some birds' feathers. She is an expert about everything on Bird Island and is proud of the island's history. Stella loves leading tours of the island, but is happy to hand over the reins if someone needs to fulfil an anger-management assignment.

ALL ABOUT STELLA

OCCUPATION: Official tour guide for Bird Island!

FAVOURITE COLOUR: Pink!

FAVOURITE BOOK: *101 Parkour Moves*.

SPECIAL SKILLS: Parkour and Bird Island expert.

HOBBIES: Giving amazing tours, hanging out with my friends and practising my parkour moves!

FAVOURITE PLACE ON BIRD ISLAND: Everywhere! I just LOVE this island!

BEST FRIEND: I'm BFFs with everyone!

GREATEST WISH: Happiness for every bird all the time!

BIGGEST FEAR: Unhappiness. And bad-feather days.

WHAT MAKES YOU HAPPY? Just about everything, but especially spending time with my friends and giving tours of Bird Island!

WHAT MAKES YOU ANGRY? Oh I never get angry, silly!

MOTTO: Hug today just like you hugged yesterday!

SHIRLEY

Shirley is the oldest bird on the island. It takes her a long time to get around! She manages to always be out and about Bird Village, especially when other birds are in a hurry. If you help her cross the road, she'll likely share a story about the good old days.

ALL ABOUT SHIRLEY

OCCUPATION: Oh goodness, I am long retired.

FAVOURITE COLOUR: Yellow, I think. Or it could be light blue. I don't remember, dearie.

FAVOURITE BOOK: *I Know Why the Caged Bird Sings* speaks to my heart.

SPECIAL SKILLS: Oh, these days I'm just happy making it across the street in less than an hour.

HOBBIES: Knitting, crocheting, watching daytime TV, shopping and taking a nice stroll through the garden.

FAVOURITE PLACE ON BIRD ISLAND: My hut has been home to me for many years, so I like it there best.

BEST FRIEND: Officer Beakins. He always helps me cross the road.

GREATEST WISH: A new set of wheels and maybe a horn for my walker.

BIGGEST FEAR: Not making it home for my favourite show, *The Bird and the Beautiful*.

WHAT MAKES YOU HAPPY? Oh, pretty much every day is worth celebrating.

WHAT MAKES YOU ANGRY? I'm too old and tired to be angry. My, what a question!

MOTTO: Help an old lady across the street, will you?

HAL

Hal is a bongo-playing bird about town. He occasionally helps out at Matilda's Infinity Acceptance Centre. Hal's specialty is any class where a steady beat is needed. Hal is known as the "boomerang bird" due to his large beak.

ALL ABOUT HAL

OCCUPATION: Percussionist.

FAVOURITE COLOUR: Red-hot jazz.

FAVOURITE BOOK: *The Tin Drum*.

SPECIAL SKILLS: Playing a duet. Soothing Angry Birds through music.

HOBBIES: Playing and writing music.

FAVOURITE PLACE ON BIRD ISLAND: Anywhere I can play my bongos, which is pretty much anywhere.

BEST FRIEND: Bubbles.

GREATEST WISH: To form a marching band.

BIGGEST FEAR: Misplacing my bongo set.

WHAT MAKES YOU HAPPY? The beat of my heart synching up with the beat of my drum.

WHAT MAKES YOU ANGRY? Missing a beat.

MOTTO: March to the beat of your own drum. But if you don't have a drum, march to the beat of mine!

BUBBLES

If you hear the sweet sounds of a horn, chances are Bubbles is nearby. Like Hal, this popular island musician keeps the island birds entertained with the toot of his horn. He also lends his talents to the Infinity Acceptance Centre. Bubbles does best in classes where calming sounds are needed. He can literally blow up to more than three times his normal size when he's excited or surprised, as the Hug Trader recently discovered. Talk about a big squeeze!

ALL ABOUT BUBBLES

OCCUPATION: Musician.

FAVOURITE COLOUR: The blues.

FAVOURITE BOOK: Any book about music.

SPECIAL SKILLS: Improvising.

HOBBIES: Playing and listening to music.

FAVOURITE PLACE ON BIRD ISLAND: The Birdfeeder – the acoustics are perfect there.

BEST FRIEND: Hal.

GREATEST WISH: To perform at Carn-egg-ie Hall.

BIGGEST FEAR: Hitting the wrong note during a big performance.

WHAT MAKES YOU HAPPY? Blowing the horn.

WHAT MAKES YOU ANGRY? Being out of tune.

MOTTO: A song a day keeps the blues away, unless you're playing rhythm and blues, then it's totally OK.

TERENCE

Terence is a bird of very few words. In fact, Terence is a bird of pretty much NO words! He mostly growls and groans and sighs. He's the biggest, tallest bird on the island and he also might be the scariest bird on the island as well. He's a permanent member of Matilda's anger-management class due to an unspecified classified incident. His art therapy samples show signs of a true artistic calling. But there's no indication of Terence answering that call, since he doesn't speak! Underneath all that bulk and brawn, many suspect that Terence is really just a big softie.

ALL ABOUT TERENCE

OCCUPATION: Grrrr.

FAVOURITE COLOUR: Hnnnn.

FAVOURITE BOOK: Grrrr.

SPECIAL SKILLS: Hnnnn.

HOBBIES: Grrrr.

FAVOURITE PLACE ON BIRD ISLAND: Hnnnn.

BEST FRIEND: Grrrr.

GREATEST WISH: Hnnnn.

BIGGEST FEAR: Grrrr.

WHAT MAKES YOU HAPPY? Hnnnn.

WHAT MAKES YOU ANGRY? Grrrr.

MOTTO: Hnnnn.

MIGHTY EAGLE

Mighty Eagle is the stuff of legends. Heck, he IS a legend! Heroic, brave, adventurous and strong, Mighty Eagle watches over Bird Island and makes sure no harm comes to the birds. He is the subject of songs, poems, comic books, stories and even fan fiction. He represents the very best of birdkind. Rumour has it that he can even fly!

Mighty Eagle lives far above us all in his mountaintop eyrie in the Ancient Tree by the Lake of Wisdom. He is rarely seen in public, but islanders sense his presence and are reassured by his far-reaching greatness. His intelligence and bravery are inspiring, and every bird aims to be noble and good like this legendary hero.

ALL ABOUT MIGHTY EAGLE

OCCUPATION: Hero and protector. Defender of homes and liberty!

FAVOURITE COLOUR: Clear blue, the colour of the sky from my mountaintop.

FAVOURITE BOOK: *Mighty Eagle's Book of Wisdom*.

SPECIAL SKILLS: Bravery, strength, heroism, humility and flying.

HOBBIES: Telling stories of the magnificent past.

FAVOURITE PLACE ON BIRD ISLAND: My cave (aka the Hall of Heroism).

BEST FRIEND: No one. A hero must stand alone.

GREATEST WISH: That all of Bird Island sings my praises.

BIGGEST FEAR: None. I am fearless.

WHAT MAKES YOU HAPPY? Being strong.

WHAT MAKES YOU ANGRY? Nothing. I am too brave to be angry.

MOTTO: Mighty Eagle flying free, defender of homes and liberty!

POP QUIZ!

Birdsonality Test

Ever wonder which member of the flock you are most similar to? Answer the questions below, then see what your matching birdsonality would be. Ask each of your friends these fun questions and see which bird they wind up with!

WHICH OF THE FOLLOWING SOUNDS MOST LIKE YOU?

A I'm always excited and happy at the start of each day!

B I cannot wait to start talking to anyone who'll listen.

C I wake up each day hoping there is nothing that puts me in a bad mood.

D I don't like to be talked to first thing in the morning.

E I can't wait to show everyone how brave and strong I am!

WHAT ARE THE TYPES OF FRIENDS YOU LIKE TO HAVE AROUND YOU?

A Super-fun and adventurous people!

B Those who will listen to what I have to say and appreciate my wisdom.

C I'm really more of a loner.

D Those who are just a little intimidated by my air of mystery.

E Those who are impressed with physical feats!

WHAT IS YOUR BEST QUALITY?

A I like to stay positive, no matter what!

B My wisdom and judgment.

C I'm the only one who thinks the way I do.

D My silence.

E My bravery, physical skills and heroism.

WHAT TYPES OF THINGS WOULD YOU DO IF YOU THREW A PARTY?

A Games and activities that involve everyone and have us all laughing!

B Let everyone hear stories and poems I have written specially for the occasion.

C I probably wouldn't plan a party anytime soon.

D I'd leave planning things up to someone else.

E Lots of games and activities that require physical skills, especially dancing!

WHAT DO YOU THINK SOUNDS LIKE THE MOST FUN THING TO DO?

A **Discover new places and explore with my best friends!**

B **Listen to friends' problems and give what I think is the best advice.**

C **Spend some quality time alone with a good book.**

D **Pick flowers in the park.**

E **Challenge myself with fun exercises and physical games.**

SO WHAT'S YOUR BIRDSONALITY?!

If you answered **A** to most of the questions, you are most like Stella.

If you answered **B** to most of the questions, you are most like Judge Peckinpah.

If you answered **C** to most of the questions, you are most like Red.

If you answered **D** to most of the questions, you are most like Terence.

If you answered **E** to most of the questions, you are most like Mighty Eagle.

SECTION

THEY'RE NOT MAD, THEY'RE ANGRY

While the majority of Bird Island residents are happy twenty-four hours a day, seven days a week, there is a small segment of the population that is angry. Very angry. It usually feels like the birdiverse is against them. But one time, the stars lined up perfectly and I found myself forced to spend time with a few other Angry Birds in an anger-management class. Which leads me to another of Red's Rules: *when life gives you anger-management classes, make yourself angrier.*

CHUCK

Chuck is one of the most animated birds on the island. He has more energy and speed than any other bird. And when they go unchecked, he can be very volatile. Still, his heart is in the right place, and he wants to be everyone's friend – even birds who aren't looking for a friend. He walks, talks, runs, eats, reads, sleeps and even *thinks* fast! Chuck gets bored easily and ended up in anger-management classes after a few too many speeding tickets.

ALL ABOUT CHUCK

OCCUPATION: What does this mean?

FAVOURITE COLOUR: Yellow! But I also like red. And brown. And black. And green. And orange and pink and lots of other colours!

FAVOURITE BOOK: But there are SO many! Right now I'm speed-reading the *Complete Encyclopedia of Tropical Birds*!

SPECIAL SKILLS: I can run and move and talk faster than any other bird on Bird Island!

HOBBIES: Running, dancing, jumping, singing, skipping, fencing, spinning and twirling! And I like to knit, too. You know, for quiet time.

FAVOURITE PLACE ON BIRD ISLAND: Pretty much everywhere and anywhere on the island!

BEST FRIEND: Bomb and Red! And I guess Matilda, too, although I wouldn't say she's my best friend. More like a friendly instructor.

GREATEST WISH: To run wherever I want. And to sing, dance and have everyone come to my shows that will undoubtedly be huge hits!

BIGGEST FEAR: Having to sit still.

WHAT MAKES YOU HAPPY? Pretty much everything, but especially running and being fast!

WHAT MAKES YOU ANGRY? I definitely do not like getting speeding tickets, especially three tickets in one day. That is NOT fun. I also don't like slow-moving birds, slow eaters or birds who are late.

MOTTO: Keep moving! Or run like the wind! Ooh, I could probably think up some others. . . .

BOMB

Bomb is the only bird with IED, or Intermittent Explosive Disorder. He can't control when or where he'll explode. Usually stress or being surprised triggers Bomb to detonate, but there have been plenty of times that he's exploded under more normal circumstances. Bomb has a big heart and is a gentle giant. He wouldn't hurt a fly. Well, he'd eat the fly, technically, but he wouldn't hurt it. If that makes sense.

ALL ABOUT BOMB

OCCUPATION: Yes.

FAVOURITE COLOUR: Black. No, blue! Or maybe red? I don't know. What do you think?

FAVOURITE BOOK: Any book read out loud. Listening to other people read aloud helps me relax.

SPECIAL SKILLS: Exploding, but I'm still figuring out how to control it.

HOBBIES: Painting. Keeping up with Chuck.

FAVOURITE PLACE ON BIRD ISLAND: Oh, I like Chuck's house. And mine is nice. And maybe the beach.

BEST FRIEND: Chuck is pretty great. And Red, too. Yeah. They're probably my best pals.

GREATEST WISH: To control my explosions.

BIGGEST FEAR: Surprise parties – there's usually a surprise that no one expects when I'm around – the ultimate party foul.

WHAT MAKES YOU HAPPY? Anger-management classes. They're fun!

WHAT MAKES YOU ANGRY? When other birds see me as just an explosive freak of nature. I have feelings, too!

MOTTO: Keep calm and carry a fire extinguisher.

MATILDA

Matilda runs the Infinity Acceptance Centre, Bird Island's first and only place dedicated to promoting the well-being of birds everywhere. She's also the head instructor. She has a "Free Range" certificate, which means she's qualified to teach other birds how to be less angry and more peaceful, productive members of bird society. She is a former Angry Bird, so she's clucked the cluck and walked the walk. Her goal is for all birds to leave her classes happier, calmer and more centred (with the exception of Red, but she's working on it!).

All About Matilda

OCCUPATION: Instructor of the Infinity Acceptance Centre!

FAVOURITE COLOUR: Every colour has its own beauty and its own special magic.

FAVOURITE BOOK: *The Seven Habits of Highly Effective Birds* is a very influential book for me.

SPECIAL SKILLS: Providing grounding, emotional support and nurturing talents in a non-judgemental and personal way.

HOBBIES: Gardening, meditation, yoga and being in nature.

FAVOURITE PLACE ON BIRD ISLAND: The Infinity Acceptance Centre, where every bird is welcome!

BEST FRIEND: The birdiverse is my best friend.

GREATEST WISH: To unite birdkind in an invisible web of love and light and happiness and peace!

BIGGEST FEAR: Not getting through to the birds who need me most, like Red. His anger is a daily challenge.

WHAT MAKES YOU HAPPY? Look around – what's not to love about Bird Island and our magnificent home?

WHAT MAKES YOU ANGRY? Those who refuse to listen or work towards their own happiness. It's very hard when a bird is unwilling to cooperate and deliberately makes things harder. I CAN'T STAND THAT! Oh my goodness! I lost my temper then.

MOTTO: Every bird is beautiful!

THE 5 STAGES OF ANGER

Anger is a part of life. Every bird feels it. But sometimes that anger takes over and does more than ruffle feathers. Below are the five stages of anger. Recognising these stages in yourself and others will help diffuse any situation before you're at Stage 3 or beyond.

STAGE 1: IRRITATED

Sometimes something another bird says or does, or even the mood you wake up in, makes you irritated. This is pretty mild anger, so usually a few deep breaths or doing an activity you like turns your day around and changes your mood.

STAGE 2: ANNOYED

When other birds are rubbing your feathers the wrong way and you'd rather leave before you do something you'll regret, that's officially called annoyed. A little meditation or some yoga usually will return you to your normal happy bird state.

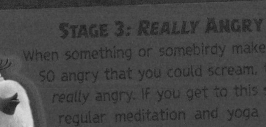

STAGE 3: REALLY ANGRY

When something or somebirdy makes you SO angry that you could scream, that's *really* angry. If you get to this stage, regular meditation and yoga won't necessarily work. You'll need the calming influence of a professional. Stop by the Infinity Acceptance Centre as soon as possible.

STAGE 4: EXPLOSIVE

This is when you are so angry you feel you might actually explode! For most birds, this is as angry as they get. Multiple sessions at the Infinity Acceptance Centre are strongly encouraged.

STAGE 5: SEEING RED

Red is so angry he actually gets a category all to himself! In all my years teaching at the Infinity Acceptance Centre, I have never come across a bird more stubborn, more furious, or more rebellious. I hope that one day he can either let go of all that anger, or learn to channel it for good!

ZEN ZONE

MATILDA'S YOGA CLASSES ARE DESIGNED SO THAT EVERY BIRD CAN DO THEM AND FEEL HIS OR HER BEST. ALL THAT IS REQUIRED IS AN OPEN MIND AND A WILLINGNESS TO LEARN! HERE ARE JUST A FEW OF THE POSES:

DANCER: This pose is best for stretching the whole body. It keeps you limber and loose so you can successfully face any obstacle that comes your way!

EAGLE: Spread those wings and reach for the sky! A noble pose for a noble bird.

HERON: Stand on one leg and maintain this pose as long as you can to achieve a state of Zen.

PEACOCK: A pose to warm up your lower body and allow you to show off your beautiful feathers!

WARRIOR: Channel your inner fighting spirit in this pose designed to show the beauty of strength.

MOUNTAIN: A quiet, still pose to channel and focus all your inner energy.

TREE: Solid, ancient and unswaying, this pose roots you in the Now.

RABBIT: Hop along to peacefulness with this challenging pose that gets you close to the ground.

FISH: Flip your imaginary fins upstream and find yourself in an ocean of calm and peace.

KING PIGEON: Stand with your wings close to your body and move your neck backwards and forwards to clear your mind of all troubles.

DOWNWARD DUCK: One of my favourite poses! Feel the stretch from the tips of your feathers to the bottoms of your talons as you release all the stress and bad energy.

PRACTISE THESE ANY TIME YOU FEEL ANGRY OR STRESSED. AND TRY NOT TO GET ANGRIER OR MORE STRESSED. MATILDA ENDS EACH CLASS WITH A REMINDER THAT YOGA WILL LEAD STUDENTS INTO SOMETHING KNOWN AS A STATE OF BIRDVANA.

POP QUIZ!

Let's Be Friends

Friends come in all shapes, sizes . . . and personalities. Take this quiz and see who just might be your new BFF (Best Feathered Friend)!

YOU ARE NATURALLY CALM AND EASY-GOING. WHICH OF THESE SOUNDS MOST APPEALING TO YOU IN TERMS OF YOUR BEST FRIEND'S PERSONALITY?

A You want to spend your time with someone just as relaxed and calm.

B You want to hang out with someone who is a bit more outgoing but knows when to keep things cool.

C You want to be with someone who is always energetic and on the go!

D You want to be with someone who is actually fun once he or she stops being a bit cranky.

YOU WANT TO RELAX AT THE END OF THE WEEK WITH YOUR BEST FRIEND. WHAT SOUNDS LIKE THE MOST FUN TO YOU?

A Going over to your friend's place to paint, draw and express yourself.

B Playing board games and eating pizza.

C Going to play crazy golf and baseball at the park.

D Just being left alone so you can relax and do your own thing.

WHEN THINGS ARE BAD, WHAT TYPE OF FRIEND DO YOU APPRECIATE MOST?

A Someone who comes over to talk with you about your feelings and helps you feel better.

B Someone who is there for you to hang out with and take your mind off your problems.

C Someone who gets you to be active and forget your problems.

D Someone who leaves you alone so you can just be by yourself.

You and your best friend are planning a holiday together. What sounds like the best holiday to you?

A A trip to a yoga retreat to meditate and find your Zen.

B A trip to explore nature and go camping.

C A trip to an amusement park to see and do as much as possible!

D Just staying around the house and hanging out and watching TV.

How often do you want to see your best friend?

A A few times a week so that you can share your latest news.

B On the weekends so you both have lots to talk about.

C Every day!

D Only if we both feel like it.

You and your best friend want to throw a party. What sounds like the kind of party you both would want to have?

A A small gathering of your closest friends to do something creative and make some fun crafts.

B A really nice group of friends to split lots of pizza and ice cream with and play a few games.

C An adventure-themed party with LOTS of activities and games and food.

D We would never want to have a party. Who wants all those people around?!

IF YOU ANSWERED A TO MOST QUESTIONS,
Matilda is your best friend! Your best friend is like you: cool, calm and collected.

IF YOU ANSWERED B TO MOST QUESTIONS,
Bomb is your best friend! You like to have fun with your best friend, but not go too crazy.

IF YOU ANSWERED C TO MOST QUESTIONS,
Chuck is your best friend! Your best friend likes to do things at full speed, and that's just perfect with you!

IF YOU ANSWERED D TO MOST QUESTIONS,
Red is your best friend! You and your best friend like to spend as much time apart as you do together. You both need a lot of alone time.

4

PIGNORANCE IS BLISS

It wouldn't be a complete picture of Bird Island if I didn't tell you about the underbelly of life here. I mean, I do try to ignore it – or specifically, *them*. But to understand the current state of bird affairs, I'll have to discuss my least favourite subject: pigs.

There are these things called pigs, and they've crashed their ship on Bird Island. And get this, they're all green! I don't trust them. Not one bit. But will any bird listen to me? No. They're all, "We love our new green friends! We're going to welcome them into our city and homes without hesitation!" Who does that?!

Especially when they have no problem dropping anchor on some poor, unsuspecting hut. Unforgivable, right? Because that's exactly what they did to my hut . . . without so much as an *I'm sorry*. I'm telling you, something smells fishy about these pigs, and I'm going to get to the bottom of it. By applying another of Red's Rules: *always keep your mfffph . . . umfff . . . pooof . . .*

Yes, well. Thank you, angry red guy with the eyebrows, for that . . . um, curiously interesting introduction. I am Leonard, ambassador to the pigs of Piggy Island.

I'd like to introduce you now to myself and my kin, and to show you the charms of our culture. I'm sure by this point you need a break from all those birds – fascinating as they may be, of course. Sit back, grab your favourite beverage and prepare to be blown away by the wonderful world of the pigs! I believe that Angry Bird was about to share a rule, before he decided to join my friends for a quick drink. So instead, how about I make a suggestion? *Just chill out. Bliss is practically guaranteed when pigs are in charge.*

PIGGY ISLAND

Ah, Piggy Island! What can be said about Piggy Island? A lot, actually, and it's all good. Piggy Island is a *wonderful* place to live, full of happy, lively pigs and the most beautiful nature, weather and scenery ever known to pigkind. It is nestled in the middle of the calm and clear ocean, not too far away from Bird Island. With every luxury and amenity a pig could want, there is not a more ideal place to live. Why, the island is nothing short of magnificent!

HARBOUR

SLINGSHOT

CASTLE

PIG CITY

CITY GATE - PURELY DECORATIVE. ALL ARE
WELCOME TO COME AND GO AS THEY PLEASE,
ESPECIALLY IF THEY HAVE EGGS.

PIG CITY

Pig City is the very heart of Piggy Island, where happy piggies
live and where our generous – and handsome – King Pig rules.

FOOD

CASTLE

PIGGY POW·A

100% PIG MUSCLE

DAZZLING
INVENTION

Pig
Fone

LOST
PIG

HAVE YOU
SEEN ME?

King Pig's castle lies at the centre of Pig City, with all the other pigs living, working and building all around the castle.

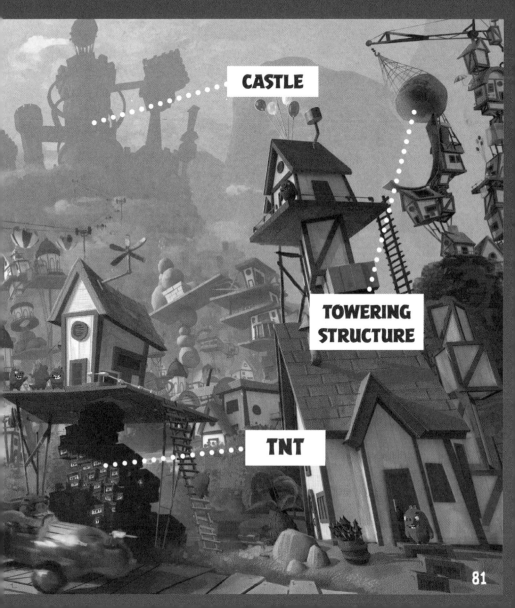

CASTLE

TOWERING STRUCTURE

TNT

PIG SHIP

The pig ship is a fine example of classic pig construction: durable, elegant and packed with everything a pig might need for a voyage. There are a few minor flaws in the design – the ramp only works about 50 per cent of the time – but all in all, it is a marvel. Plus, the pigs are working on a bold solution.

This vessel can house more than one hundred pigs, a room full of trampolines, countless copies of our favourite books and an ample wardrobe of cowboy outfits. These are all essential items for the Bird Island mission – allowing the pigs to share their sophisticated culture *and* ensuring a comfortable trip.

We pigs love to put on a cowboy show. Indeed, some of my trusty cousins only feel truly happy when dressed in leather chaps and line dancing to the strum of a banjo. That's why we always have a wardrobe full of tassels and Stetsons at the ready. Rawhide!

COSTUME WARDROBE

TNT ROOM

THE GIFT THAT KEEPS ON GIVING

Being an ambassador of Piggy Island, I would never think of arriving on Bird Island empty-handed. The pigs and I presented the lovely birds with several pig-made gifts to make their lives easier and more convenient – not to mention more enjoyable. The largest and most memorable (as well as heaviest) of these gifts is called the slingshot.

Why waste time and precious energy carrying things when they can be placed on this slingshot, pulled back and released. The sense of well-being and accomplishment is guaranteed as each item hurtles towards its destination in a graceful arc. There's nothing like genuine pig-made efficiency to make the day a little easier. The slingshot is even large enough to accommodate the birds themselves, which will make their getting around their island even faster. We give the birds gifts like these to keep them happy. Pigs are generous like that. What could possibly go wrong?

LEONARD

I am the first to admit that I am just a humble pig. I want nothing more than to be friends with the birds - a modest goal for a modest pig.

My job is a cross between an ambassador and a salespig - spreading the word about the great and beautiful culture of Piggy Island, and how that culture should be forced on— er, shared with other cultures to promote exchange and growth. It's why we pigs came to Bird Island: a rich, savory, delicious, uh, chance to exchange ideas. I firmly believe that the best way to accomplish this is by surrendering complete trust and control. It's the best way for the pig programme to work. What could go wrong?

ALL ABOUT LEONARD

OCCUPATION: Master of Ceremonies and leader of the pigs' voyage to Bird Island.

FAVOURITE COLOUR: Green. And soft white, like the colour of those lovely eggs I see all around Bird Village.

FAVOURITE BOOK: I prefer the classics, especially *Huckleberry Pig* and *Piglas Shrugged*.

SPECIAL SKILLS: Line dancing, yodelling.

HOBBIES: Fine dining, hosting parties, politics, power.

FAVOURITE PLACE ON PIGGY ISLAND: King Pig's castle is a truly magnificent palace fit for a beloved monarch.

BEST FRIEND: I think of every pig as a friend, but, truth be told, it's hard for me to find an equal.

GREATEST WISH: To unite the pig and eggs . . . I mean pigs and *birds* in a giant celebration of mutual respect and love!

BIGGEST FEAR: Not achieving my greatest wish!

WHAT MAKES YOU HAPPY? The chance to use my diplomacy skills to forge new and lasting relationships.

WHAT MAKES YOU ANGRY? Those who do not cooperate.

MOTTO: Power is a many-splendoured thing.

ROSS

Ross is my trusted associate and assistant. He helps make sure that diplomatic missions go smoothly. He's a simple, hard-working and honest fellow, especially when it comes to my cares and concerns. Attentive to every last detail, Ross will go out of his way to make me happy. Did I mention he is simple? Because he is. Very simple. Simple is probably his middle name.

ALL ABOUT ROSS

OCCUPATION: First Officer and Assistant Pig.

FAVOURITE COLOUR: Green.

FAVOURITE BOOK: *Tinker, Tailor, Soldier, Pig*.

SPECIAL SKILLS: I'm very good at assisting and first-officing.

HOBBIES: Whatever Leonard tells me to enjoy, especially sewing costumes.

FAVOURITE PLACE ON PIGGY ISLAND: My workroom, where I can tinker and create new constructions.

BEST FRIEND: Leonard, of course and all other pigs.

GREATEST WISH: Leonard's endless happiness.

BIGGEST FEAR: Same as Leonard – whatever it is.

WHAT MAKES YOU HAPPY? If Leonard is happy, I'm happy.

WHAT MAKES YOU ANGRY? Not getting food.

MOTTO: Make Leonard happy.

THE PIGS

The pigs are honest, decent, kind and incredibly dim-witted folk. If properly guided by some brilliant pig, for instance, they can do marvelous things. They like to build, sew costumes, dance, party and eat, and that's pretty much it. Aren't they so gosh darn adorable?

ALL ABOUT THE PIGS

OCCUPATION: Pigz.

FAVOURITE COLOUR: Greeen.

FAVOURITE BOOK: What iz book?

SPECIAL SKILLS: Building. Smyling. Eeting.

HOBBIES: Awl of it.

FAVOURITE PLACE ON PIGGY ISLAND: Pig Citee.

BEST FRIEND: Eech other!

GREATEST WISH: Moar food!

BIGGEST FEAR: Not enuf food!

WHAT MAKES YOU HAPPY? Food! Billding! Explosives!

WHAT MAKES YOU ANGRY? Angreee?

MOTTO: Eet? Yum!

POP QUIZ!

Piggy Edition

Have you soaked up enough pig culture yet to proclaim yourself a pig connoisseur? I would love to see how you do on this quiz about my beloved pigs.

1. TRUE OR FALSE:

Bird Island and Piggy Island are located directly next to each other.

2. THE PIGS ARE LED BY A WISE AND WONDERFUL KING.

Where does this king live?

3. WHAT IS EVERY PIG'S FAVOURITE COLOUR?

4. OUR PIG SHIP IS STOCKED WITH THREE IMPORTANT THINGS FOR ALL OUR JOURNEYS:

A TNT, toothpaste and trampolines

B Copies of *Fifty Shades of Green*, trampolines and cowboy outfits

C Cowboy outfits, fresh flowers and soda pop

D Trampolines, TNT and lemons

5. TRUE OR FALSE:

The pigs tend to be a sad, quiet bunch that keep to themselves.

And . . . I'm back. Wow, that was a LOT of information and a LOT of one pig's ego. Like I said, something about that pig rubs my feathers the wrong way. I'm going to keep an eye on him while he and his "friends" are here. No one is going to try to ruin my home while I'm around!

Wait one second! Did I just call Bird Island my home and feel really proud instead of really angry? Am I actually feeling *happy* to live here? Life on Bird Island is pretty good, but maybe all this talking has deprived my bird brain of oxygen. This anger-management stuff can't possibly be working, can it?

So remember, that last rule I had for you? Here goes: *always keep your eyes open because you never know what you might find* – it might be happiness . . . or new friends . . . or maybe there's a group of suspicious pigs that needs investigating. Whatever it is, Bird Island has it all.